A Day in the Life: Rain Forest Animals

Capybara

Anita Ganeri

Heinemann Library
Chicago, IL

www.capstonepub.com
Visit our website to find out
more information about
Heinemann-Raintree books.

To order:

☎ Phone 800-747-4992

💻 Visit www.capstonepub.com
to browse our catalog and order online.

©2011 Heinemann Library
an imprint of Capstone Global Library, LLC
Chicago, Illinois

Edited by Nancy Dickmann, Rebecca Rissman, and
Catherine Veitch
Designed by Steve Mead
Picture research by Mica Brancic
Originated by Capstone Global Library
Printed in the United States of America in
North Mankato, Minnesota. 022019 001577

**Library of Congress Cataloging-in-
Publication Data**
Ganeri, Anita
  Capybara / Anita Ganeri.—1st ed.
    p. cm.—(A day in the life: rain forest animals)
  Includes bibliographical references and index.
  ISBN 978-1-4329-4110-9 (hc)—ISBN 978-1-4329-4121-5
(pb) 1. Capybara—Juvenile literature. I. Title.
  QL737.R662G36 2011
  599.35'9—dc22   2010001132

Acknowledgments
We would like to thank the following for permission to
reproduce photographs: Corbis pp. 4 (© Kevin Schafer),
7 (© Theo Allofs), 9 (© Joe McDonald), 19 (© Theo
Allofs), 23 mammal (© Kevin Schafer); FLPA p. 12
(Jurgen & Christine Sohns); Getty Images pp. 16 (National
Geographic/Steve Winter), 23 jaguar (National Geographic/
Steve Winter); Photolibrary pp. 6 (age fotostock/Morales
Morales), 11 (Oxford Scientific (OSF)/Mark Jones), 13
(age fotostock/Pablo Rodriguez), 14 (F1 Online/Ritterbach
Ritterbach), 15 (age fotostock/Morales Morales), 17 (Loren
McIntyre), 18 (Okapia/© Konrad Wothe), 20 (Oxford
Scientific (OSF)/Carlos Sastoque), 21 (Animals Animals/
Patti Murray); Photoshot pp. 10 (NHPA), 22 (imagebroker.
net), 23 webbed (imagebroker.net); Shutterstock pp. 23
rain forest (© Szefei), 5 (LockStockBob), 23 rodent
(LockStockBob).

Cover photograph of a capybara reproduced with permission
of Shutterstock (blewisphotography).

Back cover photographs of (left) capybara teeth reproduced
with permission of Corbis (© Theo Allofs) and (right)
capybara babies reproduced with permission of Photolibrary
(age fotostock/Morales Morales).

We would like to thank Michael Bright for his invaluable help
in the preparation of this book.

Every effort has been made to contact copyright holders
of material reproduced in this book. Any omissions will
be rectified in subsequent printings if notice is given to
the publishers.

All the internet addresses (URLs) given in this book were valid
at the time of going to press. However, due to the dynamic
nature of the Internet, some addresses may have changed
or ceased to exist since publication. While the author and
publishers regret any inconvenience this may cause readers, no
responsibility for any such changes can be accepted by either
the author or the publishers.

Contents

What Is a Capybara? 4

What Do Capybaras Look Like? 6

Where Do Capybaras Live? 8

What Do Capybaras Do at Night? 10

What Do Capybaras Eat? 12

Do Capybaras Live in Groups? 14

Does Anything Hunt Capybaras? 16

How Do Capybaras Escape from Enemies? 18

What Do Capybaras Do During the Day? 20

Capybara Body Map 22

Glossary 23

Find Out More 24

Index 24

Some words are in bold, **like this**. You can find them in the glossary on page 23.

What Is a Capybara?

A capybara is a **mammal**.

Many mammals have hairy bodies and feed their babies milk.

gerbil

Capybaras belong to a group of mammals known as **rodents**.

Gerbils, guinea pigs, mice, and squirrels are also rodents.

What Do Capybaras Look Like?

Capybaras have large, round bodies and short legs.

Their bodies are covered in shaggy, light-brown fur.

ear

teeth

Capybaras have short, flat-topped heads with small ears.

They have long, sharp front teeth for eating grass and other plants.

Where Do Capybaras Live?

Central America

South America

Capybaras live in the **rain forests** of Central America and South America.

It is warm and wet in the rain forest all year long.

Capybaras live close to rivers, ponds, and streams in the rain forest.

They look for food on land and in the water.

What Do Capybaras Do at Night?

Capybaras usually start looking for food in the evening.

Sometimes they stop for a rest. Then they start to feed again.

In some places, capybaras are hunted by people.

These capybaras look for food at night when there are no people around.

What Do Capybaras Eat?

Capybaras eat grass and water plants.

They also eat fruit and tree bark.

A capybara uses its long front teeth to cut the plants up.

Then it chews them by moving the food back and forth in its mouth.

Do Capybaras Live in Groups?

Capybaras live in groups of 10 to 30 animals.

The capybaras bark, chirp, and whistle to one another.

babies

When baby capybaras are born, all the females in the group help look after them.

Capybara babies purr to their mother.

Does Anything Hunt Capybaras?

jaguar

At night, adult capybaras have to look out for **jaguars**.

Young capybaras are also hunted by eagles, snakes, and other animals.

capybara tooth
necklace

Some people also hunt capybaras.

They eat their meat and use their skins
and teeth to make things.

How Do Capybaras Escape from Enemies?

If a capybara sees danger, it barks to warn the others in the group.

Then the capybaras run away or dive into water to hide.

Capybaras have **webbed** feet and are good swimmers.

Their eyes, ears, and nostrils are on top of their heads to help them swim.

What Do Capybaras Do During the Day?

Capybaras spend the day resting on the ground.

They do not go to sleep for long, but take short naps instead.

It is hot during the day in the **rain forest**.

Capybaras lie in the water or roll in the mud to keep cool.

Capybara Body Map

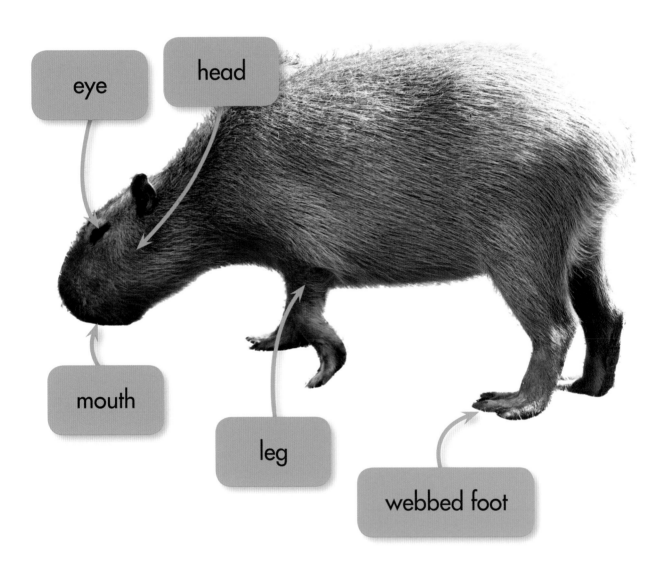

eye

head

mouth

leg

webbed foot

Glossary

jaguar big cat that is a fierce rain forest hunter

mammal animal that feeds its babies milk. Most mammals have hair or fur.

rain forest thick forest with very tall trees and a lot of rain

rodent animal such as a gerbil, mouse, rat, squirrel, and capybara

webbed having flaps of skin between the toes. Feet can be webbed.

Find Out More

Books

Gordon, Sharon. *Rain Forest Animals.* New York, NY: Marshall
  Cavendish Benchmark, 2008.
Lunis, Natalie. *Capybara: The World's Largest Rodent.* New
  York, NY: Bearport, 2010.

Websites

http://nationalzoo.si.edu/Animals/Amazonia/Facts/
  capybarafacts.cfm

www.sandiegozoo.org/animalbytes/t-capybara.html

Index

babies 15
Central America 8
feeding 9, 10, 11, 12, 13
hiding 18
jaguars 16
mammals 4
people 11, 17
resting 10, 20
rodents 5
sounds 14, 15
South America 8
swimming 19
teeth 7, 13